NARCISSIST

*How to identify and deal with the personality
trait of a narcissist. Use first-rate methods in
various life and family situations to approach
and understand the nature in both genders*

How to make a killer **First Impression** without embarrassing yourself, even if you're socially awkward and can hardly start a conversation

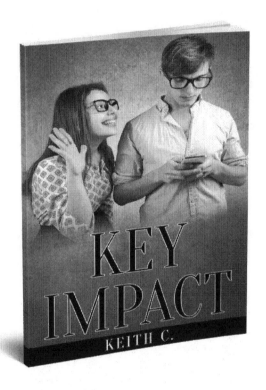

To sign up for my free author newsletter and get your free copy of the first impressions guidebook *Key Impact*, visit

bit.ly/kckeyimpact

TABLE OF CONTENTS

INTRODUCTION

In an ancient Greek myth, there once lived a handsome man named Narcissus. One day, he went hunting with his companions in the woods. Unbeknownst to the hunters, Echo, a cursed mountain nymph followed behind them. She found herself captivated and infatuated with Narcissus and his beauty. The longer she followed, the more desperately she wanted to call out to him and let him know how she felt, but due to her curse, she was unable to say anything. She had been cursed by the goddess Hera only to repeat the last thing said to her.

Through some stroke of luck, Narcissus found himself separated from his companions, and called out,

"Is anyone there?" Finally, Echo could call out. She repeated his words back to him. Narcissus called for her to come to him, only to have her repeat what he had said. Eventually, she revealed herself and reached out for an embrace. Narcissus recoiled from her embrace as he demanded she leaves him alone. Heartbroken, Echo left.

Upon learning of the story, the goddess of revenge decided to punish Narcissus for his cruelty. She lured him to a pool of water during a summer hunt. As he leaned forward for water, he saw his reflection as if he had been returned to the prime of his youth. Not realizing it was his own face he saw, he fell in love with his reflection. He remained by his reflection's side, infatuated. Ultimately, as he realized his love would remain unrequited, he discovered he could not bring himself to leave his reflection's side, and he ultimately died of dehydration and starvation. His body gave way to the flowers that now bear his name: The Narcissus flower, which we know today as the daffodil.

His legacy did not end with the flower: Narcissistic personality disorder is a very real disorder, characterized by an exaggerated feeling of self-importance, the need for adoration, and a lack of empathy. This disorder wreaks havoc wherever it goes, and like Echo was left to wither and fade away, those around a narcissist will find their own selves beginning to fade as well, drained by constantly trying to please the narcissist in their lives. These people may find themselves feeling as if their own sense of self has been taken away from them as the narcissist feeds from their attention and adoration. Many people find themselves uncomfortable with the situation but are convinced that nothing is wrong by the narcissist him/herself or those around them that do not see the narcissistic tendencies.

This book is a comprehensive introduction to identifying, understanding and handling narcissists. Through this book, you will learn the most common traits that narcissists exhibit, including why they behave the way they do. You will also be provided with how to handle narcissists in action, both by cutting off all contact when practical, and other skills when completely disengaging is impossible or undesirable. Lastly, you will be guided through healing the emotional damage from the abuse the narcissist may inflict. With the help of this book, you will be armed with all of the knowledge you will need to protect yourself from further and future abuse.

Chapter 1

NARCISSISM 101

When searching narcissism in the dictionary, you will find a result along the lines of someone who is excessively interested in themselves. You will also find synonyms of vain, egotistical, conceited, or self-absorbed. However, while these traits may be annoying, none of them are inherently harmful, and can even be healthy to the self-esteem in moderate amounts. The true narcissist, however, is much more sinister. He preys on those around him, almost unconsciously seeking out those who will fill his narcissistic supply and manipulating and abusing those who do not enable him. In order to avoid this manipulation and abuse, you must be able to identify narcissists in real time, identifying and understanding subtle behaviors that cue you to their true identity hidden behind the mask they so desperately cling to.

What is Narcissistic Personality Disorder?

The Diagnostic and Statistical Manual (DSM) 5 identifies NPD as a Cluster B personality disorder. These disorders are identified by exhibiting dramatic, hysterical, or erratic patterns of thinking or behavior. Their interactions with others are unpredictable, and most regard their behaviors as disturbing, dangerous, threatening, or dramatic at times. There are four Cluster B personality disorders: Antisocial personality disorder, borderline personality disorder, histrionic personality disorder, and narcissistic personality disorder. In NPD, narcissists are said to have an extensive pattern of grandiosity, a constant need for admiration, and a lack of empathy.

Grandiosity, in this case, is a delusion that the believer is superior to those around him or her and invulnerable to a fault. This is an unrealistic delusion of one's worth, importance, strength, influence, intelligence, or sense of self, even if there has never been any evidence that can support these beliefs as true. This is a symptom often overlooked, as people may assume this is nothing more than arrogance or conceit. It may be as seemingly harmless as exaggerating the importance of his job, or as delusional as a narcissistic spouse declaring that they are the most important person in their partner's life, and their partner would be completely lost, unable to function, and unwanted without the narcissist's generosity and kindness. These delusions of grandeur leave the narcissist believing that he could never possibly be the problem when relationships inevitably begin to fail, causing him to cast blame to those around him instead.

Narcissists, at their core, desire little more than constant admiration. This feeds into their grandiosity, as they seek to be given the attention and love they believe they deserve by virtue of being grand. As the greatest gifts to their families, narcissists believe they are worthy of constant love, attention, and praise, and when they are not praised or the center of attention, they will begin acting in ways that will draw attention, no matter how harmful or abusive it will be and with no regard to who may be hurt as a result. To them, people around them are unimportant; since the narcissist lacks empathy, he does not care about the pain of those surrounding him. So long as his narcissistic supply quota is met, nothing else matters.

Key Components of Diagnosing NPD

The DSM-5 states that in order to be diagnosed with NPD, one must exhibit at least 5 of the following 9 traits, with the traits beginning to present persistently by early adulthood, in a wide variety of different contexts and situations.

Grandiose sense of self-importance

The narcissist believes he is the most important person there is in whatever context he is in. At work, he must have the key job, and he will go through the mental gymnastics, no matter how delusional they sound to the rest of us, to convince himself that his job as a janitor is the only reason the entire building is running, or that the CNA is the only reason the patient who just underwent major heart surgery is still alive. While janitors and CNAs are undeniably necessary for their industries to keeping their businesses running, they are by no means the most important, the most difficult to replace, or crucial positions. In a relationship, she is the best thing that ever has and will ever happen to her partner. Without her, her partner would be completely helpless and miserable, or in some cases, even dead.

An obsession with fantasies of unlimited or unrealistic successes, influence, power, looks, or love

As the narcissist is the best person in the world, he deserves nothing but the best in his mind, to the point where he obsesses and fantasizes over absolute perfection at all times, regardless of how unrealistic his standards may be. He will never be satisfied unless he achieves or receives absolute perfection in every aspect of his life, which of course, means that he will never be satisfied as his standards are impossible.

Delusional sense of uniqueness

The narcissist believes she is absolutely unique or special, and therefore, she must only associate with other special people who are worthy of her attention. The narcissist will only seek out other people or institutions that are high-class enough for her, even if she herself may not belong where she believes. Likewise, those not worthy of her attention or those unaware of her perceived specialness may find themselves a victim of her scorn should they make the mistake of approaching her without her express permission. These are the people treating waiters as less than human because their sole purpose on life must clearly be to serve the customers.

A need for continuous and excessive admiration

One of the defining keys of NPD, the narcissist has an innate need to validate his or her delusions through constant and excessive attention and admiration. They seek those they know will provide this, whether it is a friend, relative, coworker, or romantic interest, preferring those whose personalities lend themselves to being empathetic because the empathetic are the ones most likely to provide the narcissist with the supply of praise, admiration, and love the narcissist craves.

A distorted sense of entitlement

Along with the belief that she is the most special person in the world, the narcissist expects to be treated as such. She believes that everything she desires will simply happen due to her being deserving of such. She believes she deserves the praise and success she wants without having to earn it.

While there is a normal sense of entitlement, in which people justify their self-esteem or expectations of success on past accomplishments, the narcissist has no such justification for her expectation.

Manipulative

Particularly in cases with toxic narcissists, those with NPD often manipulate those around them. They put up a front, hiding their true selves behind a mask and convincing everyone around them that their persona is who they really are. They are often charismatic, able to convince everyone around them, and only those closest to the narcissist find themselves victim to brainwashing, gaslighting, and countless lies that may only become obvious if the narcissist lets his mask slip. The narcissist is never wrong and will use every tactic in his playbook necessary to convince you and the rest of the world that he is not the problem.

Lacking empathy

Empathy is defined as the ability to cognitively and emotionally experience and understand the emotions or thoughts of someone else while concurrently being aware of his or her own thoughts or emotions. This is what allows us to understand what those around us are feeling, which aids in our survival as a social species. When we understand and care for those around us, we are more likely to engage in socially constructive behavior, meaning we are all more likely to survive. Narcissists lack this empathy, making it difficult or impossible for them to understand what those around them feel. With no regard for others' thoughts or feelings, the narcissist has no qualms about manipulating or hurting those around him; for her own benefit or to confirm her delusions of grandeur.

Envying others, or believing that others envy him or her

As narcissists often believe they deserve success without any effort, they envy when those around them have what they want and have yet to achieve.

He may be unable to compliment or congratulate a friend or loved one when they have succeeded, instead of detracting from the success by minimizing what was done or shifting attention back to the narcissist. For example, if his friend just bought a house, the narcissist may shrug it off and say most people buy houses, and that 15% down payment was nothing; it would have been impressive had he paid cold hard cash for the house instead of getting a mortgage. Besides, the bank currently owns the house until it is paid off, so is buying really any different than renting with extra responsibilities in the short term? At least the narcissist is renting, so when the roof needs to be replaced or the plumbing fails, the narcissist doesn't have to pay for it. The narcissist may then go on to tell himself that the friend secretly envies him because renting is so much less stressful than owning. In his mind, he tries to shift his own envy around into the other person envying him instead.

Haughty and arrogant behavioral patterns or attitudes

The narcissist may come across as haughty and arrogant, or otherwise aggressive when discussing those she believes are less important than herself. Watch interactions with waiters, cashiers, or others in service fields: The narcissist will jump on the opportunity to ream a waiter for dropping something. Not only will she behave in condescending, abrasive ways, but she may also take an offensive stance, such as standing upright, quick, sharp movements, or hands on the hips. The narcissist will often enjoy this process as well; it feeds into her delusion that she is superior to the other person; pair this with the lack of empathy and the attack can be ruthless and unending.

Behavioral Habits of Narcissists

While the presence of the previously listed traits is required to diagnose one with NPD, there are other habits or tendencies that are telltale markers of a narcissist in action. These may not be defining factors of what it means to have NPD, but they are equally as important when it comes to spotting a narcissist in real life. These are a few of the most common behavioral habits narcissists will often exhibit.

Unconstructive criticism

While criticism on its own is typically healthy and constructive, the narcissist employs it in order to put you down instead of help you improve. Rather than pointing out a flaw in your thoughts or actions in order to offer genuine insight, the narcissist will demean you in order to make you work harder to satisfy him. Even in the absence of any real flaw, the narcissist may make one and gaslight you into believing it simply to make you insecure. Meanwhile, any good qualities or successes will be ignored or disregarded, or potentially undermined and minimized. The purpose of this is to leave you feeling unworthy, insecure, and as if you are not enough to be successful or to satisfy those you love.

Playing the unwanted devil's advocate

The narcissist thrives off of chaos and leaving you feeling insecure and flustered, as when you are flustered, it feeds the narcissist's grandiosity. In order to do so, the narcissist may take absurd stances on issues that may be quite personal to you, simply to minimize your beliefs, distract you from the original argument, and cause you emotional harm. Unlike in actual cases of using the devil's advocate, which works to add to a discussion, the narcissist aims to create chaos. For example, if you recently had to put down a dog and have been grieving, the narcissist may dismiss your feelings, saying that you should be grateful that your pup passed away painlessly through euthanasia instead of dying some traumatic, violent way, and then change the subject to discussing how euthanizing humans is wrong and the doctors who aid in physician-assisted suicide are murderers. The whole purpose of this exchange is to hit you where it hurts, flip the conversation around, and suddenly imply that you and your vet murdered your dog by having him euthanized. This may leave you doubting yourself, your decision, and your core values while exacerbating the grief you already are feeling.

Malignant sarcasm

Unlike sarcasm used playfully, this sarcasm seeks to demean and hurt you. These comments may poke at your appearance or something else that the narcissist clearly does not approve of, and is often followed up with "I was just kidding!" if anyone dares call the narcissist out. For example, a narcissistic mother-in-law may look at her daughter-in-law's newly postpartum body and quip, "When's the next one due?" or something else meant to highlight the fact that her body has not yet snapped back to pre-baby size, and when called out, she may laugh it off, call it a joke, and say the daughter-in-law is too sensitive, and she meant she hoped they would have children close in age to one another. The aim of this is to inflict emotional harm and breed self-doubt, while having plausible deniability when confronted, in hopes of the sarcasm being brushed off as an abrasive personality rather than a symptom of NPD.

Verbal abuse

The narcissist may engage in name calling or other verbal abuse, aiming to degrade your sense of self, knowing that the more you hear the abuse, the truer the names and criticisms become to you. As you internalize the name-calling, the narcissist has assured another way to control your behavior. By degrading your identity and your self-esteem, you become an easier target who will be more inclined to do whatever is asked of you in hopes of getting a few scraps of validation from the narcissist in your life.

Guilt trips

Narcissists everywhere use guilt trips in order to keep their victims in line. So long as they get what they want, they do not care what cost their victims will pay. They will intentionally push buttons they know work to keep their victims following every order because they feel entitled to what they want. By knowing enough about you to know what you are insecure or sensitive about, they will find ways to coerce and guilt you into obedience. For example, if you are sensitive about being called selfish, your narcissistic best friend may declare, "Wow, you're so selfish! Remember when I bought you that thing you really wanted when I was broke? I shouldn't have done that; maybe then, I would have the money I'd need for that coffee I really want," followed by a sigh and walking away. This leaves you stuck in between a rock and a hard place; either you give in to please your friend out of obligation, even if you are in no position to spend the money, or you deny the narcissist and are suddenly selfish.

Control

The narcissist will seek to gain as much control over your life as possible, as control is power, and he believes he is deserving of it. He will seek to control every aspect he can; crying, utilizing guilt and telling you what you want to hear in order to keep you in line, and when that does not work, he will resort to name-calling, abuse, and anything else he can think of to keep you under his thumb. After all, he chose you as his target for a reason, and you are valuable to him as a commodity. While trying to keep you, he will also seek to sabotage other relationships that may pull your attention away from him. By eliminating his competition, he has free reign over you. In romantic relationships, he may dominate all decisions for your relationship, finances, and social interactions. If you resist, you will be met with either anger or guilt trips.

Comorbidity with NPD

Comorbidity occurs when two or more disorders occur at the same time. With NPD, other mental health disorders are common. The most common is borderline personality disorder (BPD), depression, eating disorders, and substance use and abuse.

Borderline personality disorder

Someone suffering from BPD often has low self-esteem. He often exhibits extreme or inappropriate reactions to emotional situations, is impulsive, and has a history of failed, unstable relationships due to the other symptoms. BPD often causes feelings of emptiness or aloneness, and people suffering from BPD fear being abandoned and rejected. They will often volatilely react if they perceive they are being abandoned. These people crave love and intimacy, but their volatile emotions often damage relationships. It is estimated that nearly 40% of people with BPD also have NPD.

The narcissist with BPD seeks to keep those they love close and react strongly at separation or perceived abandonment. As those with BPD and NPD seek contact with others for their narcissistic supply, they crave closeness and intimacy but have a tendency to manipulate others, leading to the destruction of relationships.

Depression

Particularly for the vulnerable variety, narcissists are haunted by their own insecurities and low self-esteem constantly; they do not feel comfortable with themselves, so much so that they pretend to be someone else. They rarely or never make meaningful connections with other people and live primarily to sustain themselves on their narcissistic supply. When they feel slighted, disrespected, or as if they have failed, they are likely to either fall into a depressive state or into a rage. It is no surprise that these people are frequently diagnosed with depression. They are also less likely to seek treatment, as they believe they are too perfect to need fixing.

Eating disorders

Female narcissists in particular, and sometimes males, are prone to eating disorders. For the female narcissist, her body is likely one of her primary tools for manipulating others, and she expects it to be in top condition at all times at all costs. Narcissists expect perfection from themselves and they will go to great lengths to achieve it, including falling into disordered eating to get the body they desire or that they think they deserve, even though this ultimately makes them unhealthy when unchecked. They think it is entirely within their control and that the eating disorder will never get bad enough to be dangerous, as they believe they are infallible.

Addiction

As if to cope with their true selves, narcissists often turn drugs. They have no particular preference in drugs compared to the general population, but because they believe they are infallible and perfect, they are more likely to engage in reckless or risky behavior. Narcissists believe addiction is impossible for them; they are simply too different and in control to fall victim to their brain's dependency on a substance that alters their minds. They may take a larger amount of the substance, believing they can handle it, or they may use more frequently and pair their use with driving or other activities that are dangerous under the influence.

The core delusions of grandeur and belief that they are infallible, are at the root of NPD. Add fuel to the fire, and they believe the negative consequences will never happen to them. Likewise, the narcissist will be unwilling to admit when they do fall into an addiction, as admitting would be actively acknowledging they are imperfect. They instead believe everything is fine and continue to use in the same way they have before, in denial that there is any problem.

In typical programs focused on treating addiction, one of the steps is admitting powerlessness. Narcissists refuse to submit to this. They believe they are perfect as they are, superior to those around them, and when they do admit that the drug use may be out of control, they believe they can fix it on their own. They disregard that ultimately, their brain's chemistry and dependencies rule their lives, instead of believing that if they will breaking their addiction enough, it will happen.

Chapter 2

TYPES OF NARCISSISM

NPD is by no means a one-size-fits-all diagnosis. It is a spectrum. Some narcissists are more harmful and toxic while others are somewhat harmless. Some narcissists are obvious, and others are more subtle. Understanding the differences between these varying kinds of narcissism is key for understanding how each should be handled.

Vulnerable Narcissist

Vulnerable or covert narcissists are typically more sensitive than their grandiose counterparts. Vulnerable narcissists are so caught up in fearing rejection or abandonment that they constantly swing between feeling superior to those around them to inferior based upon what is happening at the moment. During times of inferiority, they seek validation from others in order to boost their egos. Oftentimes, these narcissists are hiding their low self-esteem; projecting a persona of the victim. The vulnerable narcissist is always the victim, always demanding sympathy, and always seeking to make those around them see them as perfect. They often appear as quiet and calm, though they also struggle with emotional regulation.

Behind their narcissistic mask lies a person so broken, ashamed, and self-conscious that they put on a front to pretend to the world that they are perfect. These people seem to be overcompensating for their negative feelings and less-than-stellar view of self-worth, often due to trauma suffered in early childhood. Just like the other forms of narcissists, people who develop this form of NPD often do as a coping mechanism to handle any neglect, abuse, or trauma they faced as children. They develop a persona that is perfect, always fixating on doing things exactly right. If they are perfect, they can deny that anything bad that happens is their fault and they can develop an identity encompassed in a victim mentality. They crave the attachment or love they lacked had as children, and fear the abandonment they faced so much that they will do anything to garner the sympathy needed to keep people nearby.

These people care greatly about how those around them perceive them and will go out of their way to build rapport, and even apologize if they think it will get them the desired results. They pride them- selves on being seen as outstanding members of their society, but every good deed they do is solely to continue being seen as perfect and receiving the admiration and attention that goes hand in hand with doing good deeds. These are the people who will only do something selfless or generous if there is an audience, or will always, without fail, post their good deeds on social media for people to see. They are more likely to aim for very public careers that leave them engaging with people on the regular, usually in a context where they provide aid to others, as this feeds their need for attention, and also makes them appear to be great, upstanding people.

Unlike most of those with personality disorders, vulnerable narcissists are one of the only people who will make threats to harm themselves in order to get attention from those around them, though they will rarely follow through with their threat. These people seek sympathy through any means necessary to get their narcissistic supply, and because of this, they are often emotionally draining. They demand plenty of emotional investment while being quite sensitive as well, making those around them walk on eggshells out of fear of setting off the vulnerable narcissist.

When threatened, the vulnerable narcissist will become quite passive aggressive, as it is never his fault something went wrong. He will passive-aggressively shut out those that threaten him, with comments such as a dejected, "Well, if I am such a big bother, I'll just never go out of my way to talk to you again," fishing for you to either try to convince him that he should stay with you and that you want him there and in his life, or to agree with him, which gives him more material to use to play the victim and garner sympathy from others. When challenges continue, the vulnerable narcissist is much more explosive than the grandiose narcissist, internalizing the feelings and lashing out. The more vulnerable the narcissist, the more explosive the aggressive will become. As these people already have poor self-esteem, any threat to it is incredibly provocative.

Vulnerable narcissists pride themselves on being a great parent, child, sibling, spouse or whatever else they identify themselves as. For those who live with the narcissist, they likely often hear people say they are so lucky to have the narcissist in their lives, and the person is stuck feeling confused; no one is ever good enough for the narcissist, and the narcissist will be sure to make that clear. Growing up with a narcissistic parent, the child is constantly told he is lucky, but at home, he is constantly criticized. The end result is the child believing that he must be the problem if everyone else thinks his parents are fantastic. This is just the beginning of the damage inflicted by narcissists; the child starts life with a deep-seated belief that there is something inherently wrong with him.

Grandiose Narcissist

Unlike the vulnerable narcissist, the grandiose variety knows that he is better than everyone else and is unafraid of acting as such. These people are much less sensitive than the vulnerable narcissists and do not care as much about what other people think. They are confident, loud, and have high self-esteem, even if it is unwarranted. They are always the hero of every story, and anyone that ever wrongs them is obviously wrong. For the grandiose narcissist, if someone thinks he is less than stellar or disagrees with his stance on something, obviously that person is a plebeian that is too stupid to understand and appreciate genius, and therefore, their opinion means nothing. Anything that critic says will be disregarded as unimportant and untrue.

Likewise, in relationships, the grandiose narcissist does not care if his partner likes him. He does not care about his partner at all, only seeking to use the other person until they are no longer useful. If his partner does not admire and respect him in the way he is so confident he deserves just by virtue of being the perfect, most important, most superior person he knows, he is willing to drop everything and move on to the next victim. He also may have a penchant for indiscreetly carrying multiple affairs, not caring when his primary partner discovers the truth. In fact, he may also accuse his partner of being the one having affairs, or even get angry at his partner when called out.

These narcissists are loud about their achievements, domineering, oftentimes aggressive about getting what they want, and have no qualms about using and hurting people to get what they know they deserve. They brag about every little success that makes them appear better than those they speak to, oftentimes putting down the listener at the same time. The grandiose narcissist will not apologize, even if it will make him look better because he does not care about other people. In his mind, apologizing is something only equals or superiors deserve, and since he is obviously the best person, those he wrongs do not deserve anything.

In contrast with the vulnerable narcissist, who is overcompensating by creating a persona to garner attention and sympathy to validate her self-worth, the grandiose narcissist is not compensating for anything. He is acting on his belief and expectation that he is superior, and he should be treated as such. He may have been told throughout his entire childhood that he is superior to those around him or treated better due to social status or intelligence, and he comes to expect that treatment to carry over into every aspect of his life. He could have been top in his class or the varsity football captain and treated like royalty in school, and he held the expectation that that admiration would follow him for the rest of his life.

The grandiose narcissist thinks that if he believes something, it will become true, regardless of how disordered the thought process is. He will absolutely find some illogical way to justify his beliefs, and he will absolutely believe it. Like children, who will try to wish things into reality, the grandiose narcissist will believe their desires will happen. In their minds, there is absolutely no possible way they are wrong. If you try to provide evidence to support the fact they are wrong, they will brush you off, claiming that what you say is little more than opinion, and deny it has any plausibility. He will also do anything in his power in order to defend his belief and make his desires come true. They will not take no for an answer and will go to extreme lengths to get what they want.

Interestingly, despite grandiose narcissists believing they are much better than everyone else and expecting things to go their way, they are much more flexible when dealing with conflict. Where the vulnerable narcissist erupts into a rage at things not going as expected, the grandiose narcissist makes what he wants to happen. The grandiose narcissist will exploit and manipulate anything necessary in order to get the results he wants, even if that means upholding delusional beliefs that something went exactly according to plan. They are so confident in themselves as they present their own view of reality that they convince some people around them to believe the same.

This may be the ex-husband who cries to everyone about how much he wanted to be involved in his children's lives, but his monster of an ex-wife poisoned their minds and kept them away from him when in reality, he abandoned his children and has been avoiding their calls and attempts at contact. Despite the fact that he abandoned them, he believes wholeheartedly that his spouse alienated his children from him and shifts all of the blame to her. After all, he has always been a fantastic father and his children adored him. Those around him will take his words at face value, unaware that he simply no longer found his children useful now that they were old enough to question him, and he himself will believe the delusions he has declared. These narcissists are so convincing in their manipulation that they even manage to manipulate themselves into believing their delusions.

Malignant Narcissist

While some narcissists are little more than annoying and exhausting to interact with, a small percentage are downright toxic. These are known as malignant narcissists, and they are utterly vicious, destructive, and inhumane. These people teeter somewhere between both NPD and ASPD, often embodying all of the identifying traits of narcissists with some of ASPDs antisocial behavior tendencies, along with sadistic tendencies and, oftentimes, paranoia. These narcissists thrive off of inflicting pain and torment wherever they go.

Described by some as the epitome of evil, these people are the quintessential villain who wants nothing more than to watch the world burn. These people, though they present as grandiose and charming, have a fragile ego and are sensitive to any sort of criticism. They feel an intense desire for recognition, and they envy those around them that have the success they desire. They work hard to achieve success and present themselves as successful, though this is solely to get the admiration they desire. In reality, however, deep within themselves, they feel crushing self-doubt, inferiority, and emptiness, and they feel paranoid that their true selves will be discovered, or even worse, that others are actively seeking to expose them.

These narcissists are outwardly charming and sometimes promiscuous or seductive, but despite this gravitation toward physical intimacy with others, they are unable to develop any truly meaningful relationship. Any relationship pursued is for their own self-interest, and when they have satisfied whatever desire they had, they suddenly shift to cold and apathetic toward whoever was being used.

As seen in antisocial personality disorder, the malignant narcissist vehemently dislikes social conventions, and as such, tends to lie and steal. They have a blatant disregard for the law, and may even commit violent crimes or form terrorist organizations. These antisocial tendencies lend themselves to acts of violence or sadism, which is little more than a way of self-affirmation. By hurting and destroying those around him, the malignant narcissist feels gratification. They lack any and all forms of empathy for others, unlike other narcissists, who may feel some reduced capacity of empathy, but are still capable of feeling regret or remorse.

While manipulation is a key feature of all narcissists, those with malignant narcissism are actively seeking to manipulate others, intentionally honing their skills and calculating every move to get exactly what they want. The malignant narcissists are much more forceful in their attempts to manipulate, even if their forcefulness comes with a cost of decreasing how subtle the attempts are. Unlike how many other narcissists' opportunistic manipulation, the malignant narcissist proactively manipulates others, enjoying the process almost as much as enjoying the suffering the victim feels.

Like all narcissists, the malignant narcissists crave attention; this is a vital form of emotional and mental nourishment for them. Unlike other narcissists, however, malignant narcissists have no preference between positive or negative attention. They do not care what other people think about them, so long as other people are actively thinking about them. A negative thought about them is still good enough, and sometimes, these people will intentionally play the villain in order to garner negative attention intentionally.

The malignant narcissist is the most toxic form of narcissism there is, and these people should be avoided if at all possible. They love to cause suffering, reveling in the pain of others. They intentionally inflict harm with no regard for suffering or social conventions and do what they want when they want. These narcissists are dangerous and do not have the mental capacity to keep them from hurting, or even killing, their targets if they desire to do so.

Chapter 3

WHY DO THEY DO THAT?

Narcissists everywhere have various techniques and criteria that they use to determine their next victims. While much of the process becomes automatic, narcissists behave in predictable manners, if you know what to look for. They will seek out certain kinds of targets, and they will use specific techniques to manipulate others into doing their bidding. By understanding how they work, you will begin to understand why narcissists behave the way they do.

The Narcissist's Target

You have something desirable

Narcissists always have an ulterior motive behind everything. If you have something desirable, such as money, power, or a lavish lifestyle, the narcissist will be attracted to you. He will want whatever you have that caught his attention, and sometimes, if the stars align for the narcissist and you exhibit other traits that make you more vulnerable to manipulation, you will be an easy target for him, and he will pursue you, utilizing all of the tools at his disposal to get what he wants.

You are empathetic and compassionate

Narcissists seek those who are empathetic and compassionate. People who are compassionate and empathetic make for natural caretakers, who are a steady stream of narcissistic supply. The narcissist appears as needing compassion, and you are happy to provide it, nurturing her and doting on her, not realizing that this is what the narcissist is seeking. The narcissist is an emotional vampire, and those exuding compassion and empathy provide a nearly endless well of the narcissist's addiction. The narcissist uses this empathy and caretaker's nature to manipulate the target, constantly shifting the blame off of the narcissist and onto you, especially if you overstep when trying to care, such as attempting to provide constructive criticism gently.

Your upbringing was dysfunctional

Narcissists love people who were raised in dysfunction. If you grew up in a dysfunctional family, you have a hard time recognizing healthy boundaries and are more likely to ignore when you instinctively feel something is wrong. While boundaries are healthy, narcissists hate them. They draw a line that would prevent control and manipulation. The narcissists identify easier targets by seeking people who struggle with boundaries due to their past. Unhealthy or nonexistent boundaries allow for greater levels of manipulation.

You have low self-esteem

People with low self-esteem are easy targets because they have an innate desire to be loved, but feel as though they do not deserve it. They desperately want to find someone who loves them and will cling to any affection shown, even if there are red flags. The whirlwind romance the narcissists love to employ is a drug to those with damaged self-esteem; they are intoxicated and addicted by the intensity of the love, mistaking the narcissist as passionate as opposed to manipulating. Inevitably, the intensity of love bombing begins to wane, and the target is left yearning for the love that has faded, chasing after the narcissist in hopes of rediscovering the person the target fell in love with.

You are non-confrontational

As the narcissist employs all sorts of manipulation tactics, he naturally gravitates toward people who are hesitant to make waves by calling out any discrepancies noticed. Non-confrontational individuals will do anything necessary to keep the peace, which ironically makes them ideal targets for a narcissist. These people, who desire a peaceful life, attract some of the most conflict-driven, manipulative people in the world because of the extremes they will go to in order to cling to the peace.

The Narcissist's Toolbox

Narcissists are manipulative by nature; whether consciously or automatically, one of the key features of NPD is manipulating others in order to get what is desired. Most people do not take kindly to being manipulated, so as a reply to this, narcissists everywhere have developed tactics to sneak their ways into your life, sink in their claws, and remain there. This manipulation is typically subtle, and while you may instinctively feel that something is wrong, you cannot quite place a finger on it. By learning the most common tactics narcissists employ, you will be able to name what happened and not fall victim to the narcissist's attempts to deceive and manipulate you.

Love bombing

Especially in romantic relationships, narcissists rely

on love bombing to plant themselves in the hearts of their targets. Love bombing refers to the way in which narcissists manipulate their victims into liking them; after all, if they showed their true selves from the beginning, no one would ever willingly remain around them. In the beginning, the narcissist will provide plenty of praise, flattery, and affection in order to draw you in. Everyone loves to hear how special, unique, or beautiful they are; it is not something that people typically hear often, and the ego boost can be quite addictive, especially to those with lower self-esteem.

The love bombs ramp up over time, becoming more frequent and over-the-top, aiming to draw your attention to the narcissist and away from anyone else in your life. This isolation tactic serves to addict you to the narcissist and makes you crave being near them more than anyone else, and as you gravitate toward the narcissist more and more, the efforts double down. You talk to the narcissist more and feel as if he really knows how to listen to you. He asks all the right questions and says all the right things, and you find yourself thinking that this person seems perfect; he cares about you and seems sensitive and kind.

In reality, the narcissist wants to learn who you are so he can use your deepest insecurities and past trauma, along with what you really want in a relationship so he can use it to manipulate you.

Mirroring

Simultaneously while love bombing, narcissists employ a technique referred to as mirroring. This is when they look to you and reflect your identity back to you. The narcissist learns your likes and dislikes, agrees with everything you say, adapts your hobbies, and is generally very likable to whoever is being mirrored. As the narcissist hides his true self behind a persona, it comes as no surprise that he would choose to reflect his target. After all, most people generally enjoy those similar to themselves.

Most people do engage in some level of mirroring, unconsciously reflecting back energy level, expressions, or tone in order to build rapport with the other person and show you empathize with them. This is healthy and normal, and something we do as social species. However, narcissists take this to an extreme. They will change everything about themselves to mirror the other person.

There are three main reasons for this behavior. Narcissists lack any sort of real, stable identity, and mimic those they envy in order to get what the mirrored has. Imitation is the most sincere form of flattery, and when the narcissist sees someone with what he wants, he will copy what that person is doing in hopes of having the same results. Narcissists also may engage in mirroring because they want to target you, and therefore they present themselves at what they believe you desire in a partner in hopes of succeeding in winning your attention and affection. Lastly, they are faking the sort of intimacy that mirroring typically entails because they are incapable of any sort of genuine relationship or connection.

Triangulation

This is a dynamic in which a narcissist creates a conflict between two other people, making the people believe the other is the problem while the narcissist manipulates everything. As the name implies, a triangle of communication is created, in which the narcissist sits at one point with two other people on the remaining points. The narcissist remains blameless for whatever problem there is while the other two bicker amongst themselves.

For example, a husband caught in an affair may intentionally pit his wife against the other woman, especially in the event that the wife knows her. The husband will tell the other woman that his wife is loveless; their relationship lacks intimacy, and she had always crushed who he is as a person, and she hates him, whereas after discovered, he tells the wife all about how the other woman manipulated him and took advantage when he was drinking. He may cry to his wife, telling her how manipulated he felt by the other woman, and she may find her rage redirected to the other woman instead. In this instance, the narcissist avoids blame by both of the women focusing on one another as the problems, and he also feeds his ego by knowing he has so much influence over these women that he could completely destroy their friendship, and that he has two separate women fighting over him.

Gaslighting

This phrase comes from the play *Gas Light*, written in 1938 by Patrick Hamilton. In this play, a man repeatedly dims the gas lights in his home and convinces his wife that she must be imagining the fluctuation in brightness. Just like how the man attempts to make his wife doubt her perception, gaslighting refers to the form of manipulation seeking to make the target doubt themselves, their memory, and sanity.

By repeatedly denying whatever the target is saying or believing, along with lies and misdirection, the narcissist destabilizes the target's sense of sanity, making the target doubt everything, and believing what the narcissist says as the truth. This is a tactic to gain control over the situation. When a narcissist gaslights you, you believe you may be going insane, and over time, you begin to trust the narcissist's account. This means that if he has been abusing you, but tells you that you imagine it, you may eventually believe him.

This is a favorite tool of both vulnerable and grandiose narcissists; the vulnerable use this to maintain a relationship that is beneficial, casting aside any doubts you may have over the narcissist's intentions while the grandiose use this to convince others that what they say is the truth, even if it is not. If they say it enough, it becomes accepted. This may take the form denying that something was said, or minimizing something as less significant than it actually was, and when you begin to question them, they tell you not to be so paranoid, or may even go so far as to tell you that you are insane or overreacting.

The vulnerable narcissist may be more subtle about the techniques; if you are upset after an argument in which the narcissist said that you are incapable of succeeding, she may tell you that she didn't mean what she said the way you took it, and emphasize that all she wants is for you to get better at your job so you can succeed in the future. By twisting her own words, she has created plausible deniability in which you cannot question her intention without seeming distrustful or overly sensitive, so you accept what she said as truth, ignoring any of the red flags you feel rising.

The grandiose may brush off something as a joke, or state that what you claim did not happen at all. They may twist something around to be your own fault instead, claiming that something only happened because of something you had done.

Regardless of the form this takes, gaslighting is one of the most insidious forms of narcissistic manipulation as it breaks you as a person. The narcissist says something plausible, words things in a way that makes sense even if they are untrue, and you eventually begin to doubt yourself. You begin to defer to the narcissist for everything and take his word at face value, regardless of the glaring discrepancies you may notice.

Projecting

Like mirroring, projecting involves creating an image of something that is false. While mirroring is reflecting back what the narcissist sees, projecting is creating an image onto a blank canvas. In simpler terms, the narcissist projects by seeing someone else as someone they are not in order to fit into his own perceptions or delusions, and these projections are either positive or negative. This involves either idealizing or scapegoating people around the narcissist and is often seen the most clearly in a parent-child dynamic.

A narcissist with children may choose one child to be their "golden child," who becomes a projection of everything the narcissist desperately wants to be. The golden child is little more than an extension of the narcissistic parent in his eyes, and is treated in the way that the narcissist believes he deserves; the child may be praised, even when it is undeserved, kept protected from any sort of discipline or consequences, and is treated better than anyone else in the family. Conversely, the narcissist selects a scapegoat to project the negative side. This is where the narcissist projects his feelings of self-hate and insecurities. They are punished unfairly, blamed for things they did not do, and bear more responsibility than is appropriate for a child.

Both the golden child and scapegoat find themselves controlled and manipulated; neither are seen as their own people. They are expected to play their roles without complaint and severely punished if they try to break free. The golden child may be cast aside if he chooses to become his own person, and fearing the loss of all of the love and affection that is showered upon him, he stays in line. The scapegoat is abused into staying, believing he cannot break free on his own because he has internalized the same self-loathing and insecurities his parent has cast upon him.

While the above example involves a parent-child relationship, narcissists may also project their faults onto other adults as well by accusing them of behaving in a way they do but are insecure about. For example, a narcissist who is having an affair may accuse her partner of being the one who is cheating, or a friend may accuse you of being self-ish. This serves to redirect the narcissist's faults back upon the target; the target is so preoccupied trying to decipher whether what the narcissist claimed was true or trying to prove the narcissist wrong that the target never notices that the narcissist was the offender all along.

Shaming and belittling

Narcissists love to make others feel as insecure as they do; it becomes a form of validation in which they can tell themselves they are better than those around them because they do not feel the way you do. In order to make this happen, narcissists love to shame, although they are sure to make this subtle. Like with gaslighting, the narcissist will follow their criticism or shaming with, "I was joking, don't take things so seriously," or, 'I just wanted to help." This is used to break down your self-worth, so you get stuck in a loop of constantly trying to be good enough for the narcissist. Unfortunately, nothing is good enough for the narcissist, so this becomes a constant negative feedback loop with your self-worth becoming more and more degraded over time.

False promises and hope

Narcissists thrive on creating personas, so it is no surprise that they also say what those around them want to hear, regardless of their intention to actually follow through with what they agreed to. Narcissists do such a good job at winning over their victims in the love bombing and mirroring stages that those people cling to the hope that they can get that persona back. The problem is that the person the target seeks to find is little more than a costume that has since been discarded. The narcissist may promise to do better, to be more loving, to remain faithful in a relationship just to get back into his target's good graces, but has no intention of actually maintaining any improvements.

This works because most normal people are typically sorry when they do something wrong or hurt someone who cares about them. As a normal person, the target believes the narcissist must also work that way. However, with a diminished capacity for empathy, the narcissist does not usually see anything wrong with his behavior. This creates a cycle in which the narcissist promises to do better, does so for a period of time, and then reverts back to the previous ways. The next time, the narcissist will do better, but for a shorter period of time before reverting back to whatever behavior the partner has a problem with. In doing this, the expectations for the narcissist shrink over time, allowing the narcissist to get away with more and worse behavior that the partner eventually accepts, clinging to the hope that the narcissist will eventually return to who he first was.

Silent treatment

Narcissists are terrified of being rejected or ignored; it is their deepest fear, and as such, they employ their deepest fear as one of their favorite manipulation techniques. The narcissist uses the silent treatment to teach the individual target a lesson, though the target likely has no idea why. The narcissist suddenly falls into radio silence, refusing to look at, acknowledge, or speak to the target. At the root of this, the narcissist treating their victim as if they do not exist. The entire purpose is to invalidate you or make you feel unimportant. This comes as a shock to the victim, who is likely quite invested in the relationship with the narcissist. They are left abandoned without ever knowing why.

Intimidation

The narcissist may either veil their threats or out-right threaten or harm you in order to force you to submit to their will out of fear of the results. This can be physical, but can also be threats such as taking full custody because you are a stay at home parent who has no money or threatening to tell everyone you are a drug addict because you take antidepressants. They may threaten to cost you your job or ruin a friendship of yours, or they may take it one step further and threaten to harm you physically. This can also look like throwing objects or punching a door, or if you have managed to escape the narcissist's clutches, they may stalk you, leaving tiny signs that you know mean they were at your home, but are innocuous enough that the police tell you to stop overthinking things. The entire purpose of this tactic is to make you feel unsafe and scared of the consequences of leaving. Victims feel as if they are better off staying for, so they do not lose custody of their kids, job, or anything else.

Relationships with a Narcissist

Relationships of all kinds with narcissists follow three stages: Love bombing, devaluing, and discarding. This predictable cycle is followed regardless of the type of relationship is forged with the narcissist; narcissists will repeat this with romantic partners, children, friends, and anyone else in their lives who accept it. Those who do not accept it are either demeaned and attacked or completely disregarded and dismissed. While the three stages are followed, narcissists' behavior changes somewhat depending on the kind of relationship and what is socially acceptable within those relationship's norms.

Romantic relationship with a narcissist

A romantic relationship with a narcissist begins perfectly. It feels like it is out of a storybook about true love, and for a good reason; both the storybook and the narcissist's persona are fictitious. The narcissist works hard to draw in his target, seeking to make the target fall hard and fast for the narcissist. This is accomplished through mirroring and love-bombing.

The narcissistic romantic partner may send flowers and love notes to work every day while constantly texting their target about how beautiful they are and how perfect the two of them are together. The romantic partner may invite their target on dates constantly and will push for the relationship to move at a much quicker pace than is typical, even if the target is uncomfortable with it. The narcissist will be more controlling than the target likes, but the target will justify this as being overly-protective or due to past trauma.

Over time, as the target becomes more attached to the narcissist, the narcissist's mask begins to crumble. First it may crack slightly, but eventually, it disintegrates, leaving the narcissist in all his glory, unmasked and unbearable while you find yourself too in love with the mask to leave its pieces on the floor without trying to salvage it. With the victim firmly attached to the narcissist, the narcissist finds himself free to be himself. If he feels slighted in any way, he may lash out at the target, saying things that are hurtful or demeaning, or even yelling and intimidating the target into submission.

When in a narcissistic relationship, it is common to feel lonely, or as if you are unimportant, as the narcissist stops putting your desires first as soon as he feels you are firmly within his grasp. He no longer has to go through the effort of winning you over because you have already found yourself head-over-heels in love thanks to the intensely wonderful honeymoon period. He may move on to other tactics to keep you around, such as demeaning you or gaslighting you. You will be left with self-esteem as wounded as the narcissist's, but unlike the narcissist, yours can heal back into something healthy if given the self-care you need.

At the end of the relationship, the narcissist discards you; he may have moved onto a new source to feed his narcissistic supply, or he may have decided that the effort in maintaining you as useful is no longer worthwhile.

Co-parenting with a narcissist

Some people manage to escape their narcissistic partners but must remain in contact with them due to sharing children. The narcissist latches onto the children, with young ones serving as nourishment for their narcissistic supply while older ones are little more than a means to manipulating and hurting the co-parent. While the courts will likely order peaceful co-parenting courses, expect the narcissist to either completely disregard everything or use everything taught as weapons to manipulate others into believing they are great parents.

The narcissist does not want a healthy parent-child relationship, or will not want that relationship as the child grows older. They want little more than to do the bare minimum necessary to look good and hurt the victim that escaped them behind the scenes. This narcissist may be contrary for no reason other to cause you strife. They will follow the court order when it works for them, but will just as quickly disregard it if necessary, claiming it is misunderstood. They may drag their co-parent back to court repeatedly for no reason other than to drain money and inflict stress. They may return the children in states that make it obvious the child was not groomed or cared for in any way, or they may intentionally leave items the child needs at home just to cause a conflict and inconvenience you. They may innocently say they are running late on returning the child due to unforeseen circumstances when in reality, they wanted to mess up your plans for the rest of the day, especially if they knew you had something time-sensitive to attend to that day.

These narcissists will often triangulate, trying to alienate their children from the co-parents. They will frequently tell the child that the co-parent is at fault for anything negative, such as the narcissist refusing to allow the child to sign up for a sport or denying the co-parent to take the child on vacation and then telling the child that the co-parent refuses to sign him up or take him. They will frequently talk poorly about the co-parent in the presence of the children as well, and over time, the children may begin to believe them. Peacefully co-parenting with a narcissist is nearly impossible, as the narcissist prefers to manipulate and retaliate against the co-parent that escaped the situation. When in this situation, it is important to love your child more than you hate the narcissist, and as tempting as it may be to tell your young children the truth about their narcissistic parent, it is better to let the children learn who their parents are on their own rather than turning this into a war that the children are forced to pick sides in.

Relationship with a narcissistic parent

A narcissistic parent likely starts out as an adoring, attentive mother at the beginning of the child's life, meeting needs and performing as a perfect parent. Young children are fantastic sources of the narcissistic supply; they rely on an adult to do everything and love their caretakers immensely, ignoring any flaws that may be present. By catering to the child whenever the child needs something, the narcissist ensures that the child loves him, setting the stage for the future.

It is important to note that narcissistic parents see their children as little more than extensions of themselves; after all, in most cases, the child was created by the narcissist, and therefore literally owes their life to their parent. These parents are possessive of their children, oftentimes taking steps to keep the children dependent upon them, especially as the children grow and naturally yearn for independence. The narcissistic parent feels threatened by this desire for independence and will punish children if they act as individuals.

While narcissistic parents may seem outwardly perfect at their job, appearing as a doting, involved parent to outsiders, they lack the empathy children need. They fail to acknowledge how miserable they make their children and fail to see the damage they inflict. Parents are in a position of power, and neurotypical parents will use this power in order to guide and teach their children how to be successful, productive members of society with an end goal of the children being well prepared to enter the adult world and flourishing. For the narcissistic parent, however, this sacred trust between parent and child is abused and twisted, with the narcissist using it to increasingly control the child rather than gradually loosening control as the child matures.

These parents frequently have a short fuse and often lash out in anger. Children learn to appease their parents to escape punishment, and the only way to appease the narcissist is to conform to their expectations and constantly cater to their demands. This teaches the child that they are unimportant, and they lack the self-confidence and self-identity they will need to survive as adults. This has catastrophic results on the child and children who have withstood narcissistic parents have much higher rates of depression and low or nonexistent self-esteem.

Friendship with a narcissist

The narcissistic platonic friend makes a fantastic first impression; she relies on charm and charisma to draw attention to herself. She may have even managed to charm herself into a situation you would never have imagined shortly after meeting you, such as getting into a VIP section of a concert or managing to get a seat at a hot restaurant without a reservation. She exudes an air of confidence that attracts everyone's attention and uses that to her advantage. You initially feel so lucky that someone like her took an interest in you, especially if her reputation preceded her.

Over time, however, you begin to notice her penchant for turning every conversation and situation around to be about herself. This could be as innocuous as always being sicker whenever you are also sick or could be as over-the-top as being the maid-of-honor at your wedding and announcing that she is pregnant or newly engaged during the toasts. When attention is not on her, she may feign fainting or put herself into a vulnerable situation to get all eyes back on her.

She exaggerates her relationships to people she perceives as powerful, especially if it makes her look better or special. She appears outwardly successful in her career and has to have the best of the best, always getting the newest model of her phone or needing to have the best car out of her friends, even if it is out of her budget.

Her confidence comes with hypersensitivity to criticism, and you eventually become accustomed to this and may even find yourself specifically avoiding saying anything critical for fear of triggering her anger. You feel obligated to flatter or praise her just to keep her happy, and her presence always leaves you inexplicably annoyed and mentally drained. She may even drop you as a friend if you say something she does not like.

Whenever you need her, she is unavailable or has a much larger problem. If your mother has recently passed and you turn to her for comfort, you may find yourself trying to comfort her as she cries about how her own mother has a strange growth on her skin and she just knows it must be melanoma, and she is so afraid of losing her mother. She will constantly make your worst moments and fears about herself, and you will find yourself helping her when you need her the most.

Chapter 4

NARCISSISM BY GENDER

Both male and female narcissists must meet the criteria for diagnosis in the DSM-5; they share their penchant for vying to be the center of attention, manipulating those around them, and superiority complexes, but there are some major differences in preferred sources for their narcissistic supply and manipulation tactics they prefer to employ between the genders. Generally, male narcissists are more overt, grandiose, and generally are diagnosed more frequently than women, whereas female narcissists are much more sneaky and covert about their manipulation and typically classified as a vulnerable narcissist. By understanding the key differences in how the different genders present themselves, you do not find yourself fooled by the less overt female narcissist who creates faux friendships in order to manipulate, leaving those who do not understand narcissism to think she cannot possibly be a narcissist due to her being friendly with them. You will also understand the specifics behind the male and female's varying motivations, tendencies, and insecurities.

The Female Narcissist

The female narcissist is subtle in her narcissism; she prefers to go undetected, sucking up whatever attention she can get as needed. She prefers to be the center focus, and will absolutely use her appearance to her advantage. She often appears confident and comfortable in her skin and very embracing of her sexuality. She has no qualms over presenting herself as promiscuous and flirty in order to get what she wants. Because of this, she often obsesses over her physical self, always appearing to be meticulously groomed and carefully selecting clothing, hairstyles, and makeup that allow her to present herself as conventionally attractive and higher class. Even those who were not blessed with perfectly symmetrical features or the stereotypically perfect body appear completely confident in their appearances, a feature that many people find attractive, both romantically and platonically. True confidence is attractive to other people as when someone is self-confident, they typically inspire confidence in themselves from those around them as well.

Vanity has a downside, however, and female narcissists are much more likely to have an eating disorder than their male counterparts. This is due to female narcissists using their bodies as one of their manipulative tools. Their bodies must be perfect, and if they perceive themselves as too heavy, fat, lumpy, saggy, or flawed in any way, they fall into disordered eating in order to get their body to the proportions they deem as perfect. After all, narcissists expect nothing short of perfection.

Likewise, female narcissists take issue with aging, as the conventional beauty standard for women is achieved early to mid-20s, and once they have hit that peak, they become less and less conventionally attractive as they age. This is not meant to say that older women are less beautiful, but it highlights the female narcissist's obsession over her own self-image. She sees the hyper-sexualized ideal beauty in movies and media, and that is often younger women, and those features that make a woman conventionally attractive, symmetrical features, flawless skin, and a tight, fit body do change over time. Women, like men, begin to sag, wrinkle, and grey as the body ages, and the female narcissist sees this as the ultimate threat to her body's usefulness as a manipulative tool. It becomes something she is self-conscious of, desiring to be attractive because she believes her worth is in others' opinions of herself, and she often believes that being found attractive is the ultimate way of being desirable or valuable.

Unlike male narcissists, females are more inclined to seek their narcissistic supply at home from her family members, typically following conventional gender norms and seeing themselves as matriarchs to their families. This serves two purposes; it places them in a position of superiority and likewise grants them control over their families. In preferring to use family to validate her ego, she seeks to use her children as a primary source of her supply.

She will also tend to see her children as extensions of herself, and oftentimes project onto them. Her daughters will be more often seen as extensions of herself, whereas her sons will be put into a surrogate spousal position, in which the narcissistic mother will inappropriately confide in her son, or put adult responsibility on him starting at a young age. She will groom him to fill the role a husband typically does, shaping him into exactly what she wants. She will take credit for any successes the children achieve, claiming that they were only able to score the winning goal because she gets up at 5 a.m. every morning to make them a hearty, organic, homemade, and balanced breakfast, including using their own chickens fresh eggs and making the bread from scratch, so they are clearly getting the nutrition they require. Those other kids who lost are clearly malnourished, and at a disadvantage because their parents are nowhere near as good as she is to her children. Conversely, when her children fail or do something she does not agree with, she will make her displeasure clear, taking it as a personal insult. She may ask them why they did this to her and accuse them of intentionally doing it to hurt her. She will absolutely yell at and belittle the children that displease her, teaching them to walk on eggshells around them.

In romantic relationships, women often idealize and love bomb their target, seeking to make him or her intoxicated with her, so they want her around. She portrays herself as perfect, both in appearance and personality, and when he is hooked, and she feels like he is no longer enough, she begins to emasculate him and break him down as a person until he is willing to accept her behavior and strive to please her, and he may even tolerate her maintaining affairs with other men. One partner is rarely enough narcissistic supply, and she will seek as many sources of supply as possible, whether that is children, partners, or friends.

Females are also more covert in their rivalries with other women; they keep other women close and are very subtle about their criticism or belittling of others. In fact, their treatment of women often presents itself as a friendship if you are not well-versed in narcissistic tendencies and manipulation tactics. They seek to keep friends close, but only friends who are a little less pretty, a little less intelligent, a little less successful, or a little less rich than she is. None of her friends can better her in any way, or they will quickly find themselves discarded, as they no longer serve the purpose of making her feel better about herself and proving her as superior.

Female narcissists are much more materialistic than men and much more willing to spend frivolously. She doesn't feel the need to hoard her money to feel powerful; she loves to buy the newest, greatest tech and fashion and flaunts it at every chance she gets. She feels as if spending money makes her powerful because others see her spending this money and assume she must be rich and important, when, in reality, she is irresponsible, and may even be accruing mountains of debt in order to maintain appearances. This allows the female narcissist to feel superior without being over-the-top about it; her accessories become her social status symbols, and she never has to say a word about how great, powerful, or deserving she is, as her appearance and actions say it all.

The Male Narcissist

The male narcissist exhibits many more stereotypical traits of narcissism than the female; he is louder, more domineering, and appears more overly confident than his female counterpart. He believes he is superior to others and will assert this in any way he can, forcing others to submit to this belief. He often has much larger delusions of grandeur, in which he is the best simply because he is. Males care less about what other people think and are typically more likely to be grandiose narcissists. They seek power, control, and fulfilling their own interests and let nothing stand in their way. Power and domination are key for men, and they tend to gravitate toward more manipulative tactics and mind games as their tool of choice rather than sexual charm.

Male narcissists tend to cheat more often and are more likely to repeatedly cheat or carry on multiple affairs at one time, and seek gratification from their sexual relationships. Narcissistic men pursue multiple affairs as a way to exert control and dominance; the more partners he has, the more dominant he must be, which is the opposite of the narcissistic woman, who is seeking validation that she is attractive and desirable. He will feel powerful having multiple women at his disposal, and it is ultimately that power that he craves.

When it comes to children, men see them as an annoyance at best and competition for his narcissistic supply source at worse. Men typically use their wives or mothers as their main sources of narcissistic supply, and when children come along, naturally, the narcissist's wife will be spending ample time caring for the helpless newborn around the clock for at least a year and then spending the majority of waking hours catering to young children. Therefore, they naturally do not treat their children very well, and often assert as much control over their wives and raising the child as possible, perhaps saying he does not want to share, and therefore, she is not permitted to breastfeed, or insisting that the child is left at his parents' home for long stretches of time so he has his wife to himself. Sometimes, in the event of a vulnerable narcissistic male, he will project onto his children and actually revel in the early affection and easy narcissistic supply earned from young children, but oftentimes, they reject their children as they grow up and become more independent.

In general, narcissistic men are less likely to spend money than their female counterparts, as to them, money is power, and they want to cling to as much power as possible. That power grants them control over others, and makes them feel important or as if they should be catered to. Especially in retail or customer service contexts, the narcissistic man will see his money as justification to treat the employee poorly. His money is enough justification that he is better than everyone else. Along with this, narcissistic men love to pursue high-paying jobs that grant them positions of power and control, or if they cannot achieve these jobs, they aggrandize their own positions, looking for any justification that they are superior to their coworkers and unreplaceable to their place of employment.

Male narcissists see other men as their competition more so than a potential friend or ally; they are inclined to challenging other men, feeling threatened by their very presence, even if the other man is blissfully unaware of the threat he poses. He sees no reason to associate with other men unless it is to further his career or further dominate others. Rather than seeing any value in keeping male friendships, even superficially, he treats other men as rivals. He does not feel the need to seek validation from or justify his grandiosity with friends in the way the female narcissist does, as he is self-confident enough without it.

One specific manipulation tactic seen primarily in narcissistic men is a form of self-handicapping; when the man fears he will fail at something, he will appear confident in being able to do so, but he will find some way to self-sabotage, creating a reason as to why he cannot perform at that particular moment, or to use as the scapegoat if he does fail. This allows them to avoid failing or avoid failing without a logical reason, in front of an audience, which would directly refute his perfection. Obviously, the narcissistic man cannot allow this to happen, and instead, he manipulates the situation. The narcissist, knowing he has a very important work presentation the next day that he is not prepared for, may drink to excess, causing him to vomit the next morning, allowing him to call work with the excuse that he is vomiting. He will not explain that the reason he is vomiting is due to his own actions, and is able to avoid giving a failing presentation. Conversely, if his employer insists he comes in to give the presentation anyway, he will have an easy excuse for his failure to perform; no one performs well when they are desperately trying not to vomit on the people across from them. In this case, the narcissist either avoids performing or has a plausible, outside reason for his failure. Men are much more likely than women to engage in this behavior, choosing behavioral handicaps such as alcohol or intentionally under preparing for something. In contrast, when women do engage in this tactic, they prefer feigning illness or making up a trauma such as a friend or family member being injured or dying.

Chapter 5

TREATMENTS FOR NARCISSISM

Narcissism is particularly tricky to treat and manage; as the individual with NPD inherently believes he is perfect as he is, he is not particularly open to the idea of seeking any help to fix some flaw he does not believe exists. The pervasive denial and stubbornness make treating NPD incredibly difficult, as you cannot use therapeutic techniques on an unwilling patient, and only someone legitimately seeking to better himself will actually benefit from therapy. Because of this, NPD is largely regarded to be untreatable, especially when severe. However, for the few who are open to admitting they have a problem, psychotherapy is the most frequent treatment for narcissism. There are two types of psychotherapy that have been found effective in treating narcissism: Cognitive behavioral therapy (CBT) and psychodynamic therapy.

Cognitive behavioral therapy

This therapy focuses on restructuring distorted, unrealistic thoughts in order to alter feelings and ultimately, alter the behavior as a result. CBT recognizes the feedback loop in thoughts influencing feelings, which influence behavior, which influences thoughts, and so on indefinitely. This form of therapy interrupts the feedback loop by questioning and challenging thoughts that are unhelpful, incorrect, or unrealistic, using a variety of techniques. It is a short-term therapy with long-term results and is often quite successful when the patient is cooperative. It typically averages between 5 and 20 sessions, focusing solely on teaching the patient coping mechanisms and tools to repair disordered thoughts rather than aiming to fix any sort of past trauma that may have caused the NPD in the first place. That does not mean the therapist is uninterested in exploring any traumas; rather, the belief is that just as the reason an arm is broken is irrelevant to a doctor's treatment of the problem, the therapist is interested in fixing the current problems caused by the behavior rather than focusing on the past.

Through multiple sessions with a therapist, the narcissist gradually learns how to identify and replace grandiose or distorted thoughts with more accurate, productive thinking. This is done through journaling, homework assignments, and practice with the therapist and in real life situations. The narcissist will learn how to identify problematic behaviors and thinking and begin to deconstruct it, choosing more productive behaviors instead. As they begin implementing more productive behaviors, their thought processes should begin to improve as well, with an end goal of beginning to fix the broken self-esteem and self-worth the narcissist carries.

As a narcissist has built up an entire persona based on distorted beliefs that CBT will aim to deconstruct, tearing them down can be painstaking, but ultimately can be effective if the narcissist is truly open to receiving the treatment. Along with cognitive restructuring, the narcissist's CBT sessions will likely include behavior modification, which is learning to cease unproductive or harmful behaviors with healthier, productive actions. For narcissists with deep-rooted fears of rejection or failure, they may also be treated with exposure therapy, during which they will gradually be exposed to their most feared scenarios, so they eventually become less afraid of them.

Psychodynamic therapy

Like CBT, psychodynamic therapy is a form of psychotherapy. It is a talk therapy based on psychoanalysis with an emphasis on the patient's interactions and relationship with the world around him or her. During this therapy, patients are encouraged to discuss anything on their minds and how they feel about the thoughts they have. As the patient discusses his thoughts and feelings, the therapist asks clarifying and guiding questions that allow for the identification of patterns of thinking the patient exhibits. The ultimate goal of identifying these patterns is to lessen or eliminate symptoms of NPD by increasing self-awareness, self-esteem, which many vulnerable narcissists lack, and an understanding of why the narcissist follows the patterns in the first place. By bringing the reasons to light, the patient is able to resolve the conflicts and therefore eliminate the need to behave narcissistically.

This therapy works by developing a thorough understanding of negative or repressed feelings in order to improve current experiences and relationships. The patient learns to identify how something that happened in the past is directly impacting current behavior, and by understanding that correlation, the patient is able to begin correcting it. It seeks to bring acceptance of the past, teaching the patient to identify who he or she truly is and use that information as a way to reconfigure one's self.

Think of the person as a puzzle; the narcissist's puzzle is put together incorrectly, with pieces forced together. It kind of resembles the general colors of what the image it is supposed to present, but does not paint a clear picture. Psychodynamic therapy teaches the narcissist to disassemble the puzzle and rebuild it the way it was supposed to be. The goal here is to create a more functional identity that does not require the crutches of narcissistic tendencies in order to validate or protect itself.

Family or marital therapy

While it may be tempting to take a narcissist to therapy in order to get treatment, beware the triangulation that can occur between the therapist and yourself. The narcissist may have the charisma to charm the therapist onto her side, and if she does, you will have two people telling you that you are at the heart of all of your perceived problems. If the narcissist somehow fails to convince the therapist, then she will learn from the therapist in order to be less obvious and more convincing in the future. Just as it is typically not recommended to take your abuser to therapy with you, it is often not recommended to take a narcissist to joint therapy either. Consider this as an option after extensive individual therapy.

Chapter 6

BECOMING THE GREY ROCK AND OTHER TECHNIQUES TO SURVIVE NARCISSISM

Narcissism is difficult for anyone to survive; the narcissist harms everyone around him, whether intentionally or not, and oftentimes, the only way to truly avoid any injuries or to heal is to completely cut off the narcissist and refuse to engage in any way. However, that advice is not always practical, as the narcissist may be someone with whom you have no choice but to interact regularly, or is someone you desire to maintain contact with. In those instances, there are techniques you can use to avoid or minimize harm or to cope with the narcissist's dysfunctional behavior. Keep in mind that none of these are foolproof, and not all of them work for every narcissist. It may take experimenting to discover which of these techniques are the most effective against the narcissist in your life, but once you have discovered ways to avoid being the target of the narcissist's rage, your life will become exponentially less dramatic and much more peaceful.

Cut off

The only guaranteed way to avoid any emotional or physical harm from the narcissist is to refuse to associate with her in any way, shape, or form. By refusing to engage, you have removed the narcissist's strongest motivator; seeking narcissistic supply drives the narcissist to find those who will provide it with the least amount of trouble. By refusing to engage, you deny the narcissist the attention she needs to thrive. Just as a drug addict who will seek alternate sources to get his fix, the narcissist will soon move onto someone else in hopes of getting hers to avoid withdrawal. She may come back to you repeatedly, seeking the supply you used to provide, but if you continue to refuse to engage, she will eventually decide you are not worth the effort, or that you were never worth the effort, and therefore, you become devalued in her mind.

It is important to keep in mind that a narcissist being denied her fix often goes through what is referred to as an extinction burst; since you, at one point, reinforced yourself as a valid source of narcissistic supply, the narcissist will continue to expect you to provide it. By refusing to provide the supply, the narcissist will try a little bit harder to get her reward, and then harder, until it builds to nearly unbearable levels. They will try everything possible to get their supply fix. Think of this as a toddler throwing a temper tantrum; if you give in even a little bit, the narcissist will have confirmed that you are still a valid source of supply, so long as antics are increased, and the behavior will repeat. By surviving the extinction burst without rewarding the behavior, the narcissist will typically move on to easier sources, though they may try approaching you every now and again.

Grey rock

Although cutting off the narcissist in your life is the most effective method for avoiding emotional injuries, it is not always the most practical. Sometimes, the narcissist is someone you are required to maintain some level of contact with, and in those cases, becoming as boring as a grey rock is the easiest way to avoid becoming victim to the narcissist's wrath. This technique is perfect when you have children with a narcissist, or you have narcissistic family members who you will inevitably see on occasion at family events.

The idea behind this technique is that, during an average day, a person sees plenty of grey rocks, all of which are just as unremarkable as the next; because they are so unremarkable, they are not worth committing to memory. This technique aims to emulate the boringness of a rock, so the narcissist loses interest in you as a source of narcissistic supply while still being able to interact, albeit rather superficially.

During this method, you never respond to the narcissist in the way they are seeking. If your ex-husband texts you a rant about how horrible you are for denying him unrestricted access at all hours with his children, you ignore it. As tempting as it is to respond, you give him nothing in response. He wants you to get upset; by getting upset, you have proven that he still has control over your feelings. Only respond to messages from your ex-spouse when they ask for pertinent information about the children, such as when their next soccer game is, or what the proper dosage for their prescription is.

Likewise, your narcissistic mother-in-law may try to goad you into an argument at Thanksgiving dinner, making snide comments under the guise of joking. Either ignore this behavior, or respond with a simple, but still calm and polite, "This is neither the time nor place. Would you like gravy?" By refusing to fall for your mother-in-law's tricks and redirecting to something else, you have proven that you are not rude, and your mother-in-law gets no material to use as the victim over dinner.

Eventually, the narcissist gets bored with the constant grey rock and stops engaging altogether. They may continue to co-parent, or occasionally say something at family reunions, but you have removed yourself as a valid source for narcissistic supply in the eyes of the narcissist.

Set healthy boundaries and have consequences for ignoring them

Boundaries are healthy and normal parts of social relationships; they keep both people from stepping on the other's toes or offending them. Healthy boundaries include things such as refusing to allow others to call you names or physically hurt you; they are your way of protecting yourself, and most people have no issues respecting them. Everyone needs some degree of separation from even those they are closest to, and most people would agree that desiring to be treated with respect or not to be harmed is reasonable.

Narcissists, however, feel extremely challenged when faced with boundaries. They see them as walls that prevent them from getting the supply they desire, and as such, they will aim to stomp on every boundary you set unless you make doing so undesirable. Let the narcissist know one time that if they continue to insult or disrespect you, then you will not respond. If he calls you a name again, refuse to engage for a while, proving that it is not a technique that will work on you. Every time he continues to stomp on your boundary, lengthen the amount of time you refuse to engage with him. Tell your narcissistic mother that if she continues to show up uninvited at your home, you will not hesitate to call the police and have her cited with trespassing. The next time she shows up, follow through so she knows you are serious.

This is an important tactic to use if you have an adult narcissistic child; by installing healthy boundaries, you set lines that you will not allow her to cross. You will refuse to get her out of situations she caused herself, and you will not tolerate her abuse or attempts to manipulate you.

Take a break

Sometimes, you need to take a step back from the entire situation to reevaluate everything. This is not the same as cutting off the narcissist or punishing the narcissist; you are simply taking a time out from the relationship to give yourself time to cool off and heal from the pain inflicted. Think of this as similar to a marital separation; when separated, you are still legally married to your spouse, and likewise, you have not pulled the plug on your relationship with the narcissist when you take a time out. Instead, you are giving yourself some breathing room to heal and clear your own head to allow you to control yourself better. After all, being in the same room with someone who has infuriated you so much that you feel you need to take a step back is rarely productive, and is even less so when the other person is a narcissist who believes he can never do any wrong. When the narcissist cries to you, asking why you are so cruel to punish him in this way, remind yourself that it is not a punishment, it is self-care. You should never sacrifice your mental wellbeing for anyone, never mind a narcissist who would never do the same for you.

Never take it personally

Understand that NPD is a disordered way of thinking; the narcissist cannot help the way he thinks. By recognizing that the narcissist's way of thinking is delusional and distorted, it follows that any insults or accusations he slings are equally as delusional and distorted. He seeks to manipulate at all costs to get what he wants, and his view of the world is so skewed that anything he says should not be taken personally. Instead, brush it off as him being himself and avoid thinking anything of it beyond a quick reminder that he is unable to see the world in a realistic fashion. By refusing to accept what he says or refusing to believe what is said as true, you eliminate some of the pain and injury to your own self-esteem. As a bonus, by refusing to allow the narcissist control over your feelings and thoughts, you starve the narcissist of his supply, and he becomes less likely to use you as a source in the future.

Manage your expectations

Ultimately, in this world, the one thing we have control over is ourselves. We can choose how we think and feel. We cannot force people to change, no matter how much we may want to. By recognizing what a narcissist is at her core, you can choose to accept who she is. Understand that she has emotional limits that are not the norm in neurotypical people; she will never be your confidante, nor will she ever be a source of compassion or comfort. By accepting that the narcissist in your life has these limitations, you will find yourself much less disappointed when she behaves in a narcissistic way. This does not mean, however, that you should accept her abuse. Abuse and boundary stomping should always be corrected, but by understanding your narcissist's personality type, you will stop turning to her for the emotional support she cannot provide.

Focus on the positive

Going hand-in-hand with managing your expectations, when you seek to maintain a relationship with a narcissist after discovering her narcissistic nature, you should put an emphasis on the parts of her you genuinely enjoy. Again, do not accept abuse, but while accepting the narcissist's shortcomings, you should also emphasize what parts of the narcissist make you want to deal with the negatives. This could be the two of you sharing a hobby, or perhaps you genuinely enjoy the narcissist's intelligence. Whatever the reasons, by reminding yourself why you like her, you may find your tolerance for her shortcomings (excluding abuse) building.

Avoid calling them a narcissist

As tempting as labeling him may seem, it is almost never productive. While this is often intended as a way of pointing out a flaw in hopes of the narcissist correcting his behavior, it almost never works that way. Instead, the narcissist feels attacked or threatened and will ramp up manipulation techniques. He may try contacting you more frequently, demanding that you apologize for what you said because you are clearly wrong. No matter how blatantly obvious the narcissism is to everyone else, the narcissist does not recognize it. Labeling him is no different than criticizing him, and it will not end well.

Avoid arguing and confrontation

Just as it may be tempting to call a narcissist a narcissist, many people feel the urge to correct the narcissist's thinking at the moment, especially when the thinking is especially delusional or over-the-top. However, just as the narcissist will not accept she is a narcissist, she will also refuse to accept any rebuttal to an argument you may have. She will never accept anything that contradicts her own beliefs of the world, no matter how much evidence you provide. In the end, it is better to save your breath and not bother setting her off. Silence or a lack of speaking up does not automatically mean you agree, contrary to popular belief, and you can choose to simply let her believe what she will, even though you know she is wrong.

Likewise, when possible, avoid confronting the narcissist. If you disagree with something, weigh whether you will get what you want out of confronting the narcissist before deciding whether or not to say anything. If your narcissistic husband embarrassed you in front of your friends by drinking and then told your friends things you would prefer they not know, it might be wiser to avoid telling him how much he hurt you and instead focus on making sure he does not get that opportunity again by avoiding get-togethers involving alcohol.

Feed the narcissist's ego

Especially when you aim to remain in a relationship with a narcissist, whether romantic or familial, recognize that many vulnerable narcissists need to feel valued because their self-esteem is so fragmented. In order to bypass the manipulation stage altogether, you can keep the narcissist's ego fed, and supply met. This keeps the narcissist feeling more self-confident, especially in the case of vulnerable narcissists, and gives them no reason to go out of their way to manipulate to get the attention desired. Tell your spouse how great that meal he prepared was, or tell your mother how nice that knitted scarf looks. Little compliments go a long way for the narcissist and will help keep the narcissist happy. Instead of looking at the narcissist as some awful person who wants to be the center of attention and wants to hurt everyone around him, see him as needing words of affirmation to feel appreciated and desired. This is not manipulating the narcissist, but rather, understanding and meeting his needs by understanding how NPD affects people. Just as you would likely go through the effort to provide affection for a very physically needy spouse to meet his need for physical touch, you can choose to provide the affirmations the narcissist needs.

Chapter 7

HEALING FROM NARCISSISTIC ABUSE

Narcissistic abuse is incredibly insidious; it seeks to break you down as a person, rendering you a hollow shell of the person you were prior to the relationship with a narcissist. You may look back and wonder how you have gotten yourself into the situation you are in or ask yourself how you could be so blind. This abuse leaves you stuck in anxiety, constantly worried about what will happen next, and never feeling safe within your relationships.

If you have put up with the abuse, you must care for the person who is abusing you, and you get stuck between the dissonance of thinking of the person as someone you love and simultaneously as your abuser. Perhaps this person is a parent, someone you have expected to be nurturing and loving, or a romantic partner. Regardless of what the relationship between yourself and your abuser is, the aftermath of the relationship is undeniable. Regardless of whether you have cut off contact or you intend to maintain any level of contact with the narcissist, understand that self-care is absolutely essential to healing the wounds. This chapter will provide you with some invaluable techniques for caring for yourself and healing from a narcissist's inherent toxicity.

Acknowledge what has happened

The first step to healing from narcissistic abuse is to acknowledge it for what it really was. By accepting that the narcissist in your life consciously hurt you, and labeling it as abuse, you begin to take the blame you have internalized off of yourself and where it belongs. You were not responsible for your abuse, you did not cause your abuser to act the way he or she did, and you are not less worthy of love or respect as a result of the abuse. Remember, you are only able to control yourself. Your own behaviors did not cause the narcissist to lash out, and your own behaviors do not control the narcissist.

Instead of feeling shame from being a victim, recognize that it was largely good traits that drew the narcissist to you, and it was your good, forgiving, empathetic nature that allowed this treatment to carry on as long as it did. Narcissists target the kind caretaker people who are willing to weather the storm, so to speak, and your best traits were exploited. Rather than seeing fault with yourself, assign it where it belongs: With the narcissist. No one is ever deserving of the abuse narcissists dish out, and you are no exception. Recognize the narcissist as manipulative and abusive, and recognize that you have mental and emotional wounds that require healing. Once you have accepted that the wounds are there, you can begin to heal them.

Forgive yourself

It is easy to blame yourself retrospectively after realizing the person you trusted or loved is a narcissist. After acknowledging the abuse, forgiving yourself for not recognizing it sooner is essential. Your trust was abused and manipulated; the narcissist took advantage of your good will and used it against you as a tool to continue to hurt you. Remind yourself that you cannot change the past, but you can change the future, and acknowledging the abuse was the first step in breaking the cycle. You must be kind to yourself, forgiving yourself for allowing it to happen, so you stop beating yourself up over the situation.

Oftentimes, after discovering someone close to you is a narcissist, you immediately blame yourself for not realizing it sooner, despite the fact that narcissists are master manipulators, and most people trust what others present as themselves at face value. Instead of continuing a cycle of blame, recognize the relationship as a learning experience and release the guilt you feel. You will feel immensely better when you accept that it happened and forgive yourself for the experience.

Grieve for the relationship

After discovering someone you cared for is not who you thought; it is common to grieve. After all, you have, in a sense, just lost the person you fell in love with. Sure, the person never truly existed, but your love for her was. You did not get the mother, father, spouse, partner, or friend you deserved, and you are allowed to grieve that fact. In order to heal, you must accept the loss of the relationship you were deceived into believing, or accept that the relationship you deserved, such as a loving mother or father, did not happen.

Grief often comes in five different stages: denial, anger, bargaining, depression, and acceptance. You must make your way through all of these for your relationship in order to truly heal. Denial was the stage you were in as the narcissist's mask slipped;

you believed everything was okay and tried to hand-wave away the abuse as due to stress or other extenuating circumstances. You told yourself that the person you thought you knew was still there somewhere. Anger occurred when you discovered the truth; the person you loved was a lie. Bargaining is when you tell yourself you could stay in the relationship if only you changed certain behaviors. Your narcissistic partner would love you and treat you kindly if you avoided angering her, or your narcissistic father would be more loving if only you were a better child. You begin to feel as if offering yourself up and continuing to suffer in silence would be better than losing the person altogether. Depression sets in as you realize that the person you thought existed is not real. You feel hopeless, and as if your sadness will last forever, making you wonder if maintaining a relationship with the narcissist would be a better alternative, even in the absence of the person you thought he or she was. Finally, acceptance occurs when the depression ends, and you finally understand that this is your reality, no matter how much you dislike it. At this stage, you find yourself more able to enjoy your life and move on from the trauma.

Find an outlet for your feelings

As you have learned when discovering what makes a target attractive to a narcissist, being highly empathetic is one of the most enticing. Unfortunately, to the empaths, being surrounded by a narcissist is incredibly unhealthy. You internalize the narcissist's feelings, attempt to understand them, and, in a sense, lived in their shoes. This toxicity poisons your mind and well-being and needs to be released. After all, that is not who you are as a person. The only way to find your clarity and yourself again is to externalize the toxicity. Find outlets that work for you, whether in journaling in an attempt to understand it, seeking counseling, or finding physical outlets. Practicing meditation, yoga, exercising, or anything else that gets you moving and sweating can help you release the negativity you absorbed during your time as the narcissist's supply source.

Find support

Whether through online communities, in-person support groups, or with close friends finding others who support your journey to healing is imperative. Many people draw comfort from joining support groups of other survivors of their trauma, and survivors of narcissism are no exception. It is comforting at some level to be able to speak to others that understand what you have gone through. Not only is it validating to hear from others about their own experiences, but other survivors will also know exactly how to support you through your experience. They will understand what you mean when you discuss what the narcissist in your life said or did, rather than falling for the plausible deniability the narcissist hid behind. They will not undermine your experiences or tell you that you are overreacting, the way someone unfamiliar with the insidiousness of narcissism might. They also provide you with tangible proof that life goes on and does get better after healing from narcissistic wounds. As hopeless as you may feel during the healing process, you will see success stories that may inspire you to stay strong in moments of weakness.

In this day and age, the internet is a wealth of resources, oftentimes literally in your back pocket or the palm of your hand in the form of a cell phone. You can search for narcissistic abuse support groups in your area to find in-person meetings, and if you struggle to find something in person, there are plenty of online forums dedicated to providing support for everything from surviving narcissistic abuse to healing from a narcissistic parent, grandparent, spouse, or any other relative. Through the internet, you will be able to find others who have experience with your particular kind of narcissist, and oftentimes, people who have gone through the same experiences as you have.

Self-reflection

Oftentimes with a narcissist, you try desperately to explain away each time her mask may slip. You remain firmly in denial that anything is wrong, and just as the anecdotal frog will tolerate gradually increased temperatures until it is boiled, you will find yourself tolerating more and more of the narcissist's abuse, explaining it away, and perhaps even becoming defensive of the narcissist when other people question you on the behavior.

It is important to understand why you were tolerant of this behavior from the beginning. Maybe you empathetically explained it as a one-time occurrence, falling for the promises to do better, or you were so desperate for love that you were willing to accept it, regardless of the faults the narcissist brought. In order to understand your tolerance for the narcissist, you need to understand what the narcissist provided that you needed. Perhaps she provided the security you needed due to never getting when you needed it during childhood. Maybe he provided the love and validation you craved due to your own self-esteem issues. Maybe your up-bringing was dysfunctional, and you do not under-stand what a healthy relationship entails, or maybe you truly thought you could fix her flaws with love and effort like in fairy tales. Regardless of the rea-son, it is important to reflect on your own life and feelings in order to begin analyzing why you do the things you do.

When self-reflecting, take time to yourself in a quiet environment. Some people find it useful to keep a journal during this time. Take a deep breath and identify the subject of your reflection for that ses-sion. This could be your abuse inflicted by the nar-cissist, feelings of insecurity, or anything else. Think about this subject for a moment and begin writing. A stream of consciousness is perfect here; write out exactly what you feel or think about the subject and do not hold anything back. It is okay to cry if you feel the urge, and any thoughts, no matter how silly they may make you feel are worth writing down. Pour your feelings onto the paper, and when you feel like you have, stop. Put the journal away and continue on with your day.

Revisit your journal that night or the next day and reread your thoughts. Take a highlighter and identify key problems as you read, aiming to identify any reasons you may have been tolerant of the narcissist's behaviors. By identifying the reasons through self-reflection, you will know what left you vulnerable to the narcissist, so you know what to fix within yourself to prevent it from happening in the future.

Start therapy

Therapy is something that would be beneficial to nearly everyone, regardless of history of trauma. For someone who has survived narcissism, therapy is essential. Through therapy, you will learn to identify why you were a target for a narcissist, how to cope with whatever trauma led you to be an easy target, and how to cope with all of the feelings surrounding your relationship with the narcissist.

Cognitive behavioral therapy can be especially useful in restructuring your thoughts in order to become less vulnerable to the narcissist's clutches. It can also help you learn healthy ways to cope with stress and the pain inflicted by the narcissist. If you are having troubles locating a therapist that would be good for you, you can speak to your primary care doctor and discuss what you have gone through and how you are feeling. Your doctor can provide referrals to licensed therapists in your area in a field of therapy that the doctor thinks may be beneficial.

Engage in self-care

After spending so long caring for the narcissist, caring for yourself can seem unnatural, but it is essential to healing. You are worthy of care, and without providing it, you will inevitably burn out. This is the perfect time to take time for yourself where you do not have any other responsibilities; take an hour-long bath with your favorite book and a glass of wine, or go get a massage followed by seeing that new movie you are interested in. By taking the time to relax and do something you love, you will begin to feel more like your old self.

Take this one step further: make time daily to work on something about yourself that you wish to better, such as exercising more, eating healthier meals, or studying something you have always wanted to learn. Go back to school for a degree if you do not have one, or do anything that will help better yourself. You likely spent time being convinced that you were incapable of thriving without the narcissist around, and it is time to prove to yourself that the narcissist was wrong.

Affirmations

Affirmations are a common technique used in CBT to help change a person's negative core beliefs into something more positive. They are often meant to reverse negative beliefs and strengthen and ground yourself in moments of weakness or when you feel yourself slipping back into your old ways. By creating a small arsenal of affirmations related to your healing from narcissistic abuse, you will be able to keep your mental clarity and focus on reversing the damage the narcissist has inflicted.

Affirmations can be almost anything, so long as they meet three key criteria: They must be positive, they must be about yourself, and they must be present-tense. By keeping your affirmation positive, you keep your mind rooted in positivity and slowly teaches your mind to think in positives such as, "I need more practice," as opposed to, "I am no good at this." There is a huge difference in attitude between the two, and the positive thought lends itself more to productive behaviors, whereas the negative thought is very discouraging. They must be about yourself because ultimately, you only have control over yourself. You cannot influence other people's thoughts or feelings, and therefore, you cannot be entirely sure without a doubt that your affirmation is accurate if it involves someone else's mindset because you will never truly be privy to someone else's mind. Lastly, the affirmation in the present tense means it is true at that particular moment.

For a victim of narcissistic abuse, an example of an affirmation could be, "I trust my perception of the world around me." As narcissists love to Gaslight in order to disarm their victims, reminding yourself that your perceptions are accurate helps assuage any self-doubt that may begin to creep up, especially in situations the narcissist in your life used to manipulate. Another affirmation could be, "I am worthy of respect and love." Narcissists break down your spirit and convince you that you are not worthy of either, usually because they are incapable of genuinely respecting and loving other people.

Be gentle and patient with yourself

Remember, you are healing some major wounds inflicted by someone you trusted. This is a long process, and it is pretty typical to experience setbacks. Maybe you decided you missed the narcissist so much you contacted her despite knowing better, and you feel like all of the healing you have been doing has been undone in an instant. You feel like you are right back down in the trenches, and you are ashamed and frustrated that you erased the progress.

Instead of seeing the progress as gone forever, remind yourself that the progress was not erased; grieving comes and goes. Grieving for your loved one or the relationship you should have had will not go away instantaneously; in fact, it may never completely go away, but it does become easier to live with over time. Healing from a narcissist is a lot like losing someone you love deeply; the person you thought you knew died with the narcissist's mask slipping, and it is normal to grieve it. Instead of focusing on how you messed up, instead look back and see how far you have come since the beginning; you recognize the narcissist for what he is and can understand and identify the signs and tactics used against you for the duration of the relationship. While you may slip up from time to time, you are only human. You are not perfect, and that is okay. You are not expected to be perfect. After you inevitably fall, pick yourself up, dust yourself off, and keep going. With perseverance, you can, and you will heal from this.

CONCLUSION

Narcissistic tendencies destroy relationships. They objectify both the victim and the narcissist and reduce both parties down to good or bad, black or white, superior or inferior. If you are reading or listening to this book, you have likely been on the receiving end of a narcissist's fickle nature and have decided it was time to take action.

Armed with the knowledge this book has provided, you are ready to take your next step toward healing from narcissistic abuse. Congratulations! Acknowledging your problem and seeking out resources such as this book was the first step toward healing. This was the beginning of a long and arduous journey to mental wellness and healing from the abuse you have endured. As a survivor, you are prepared to protect yourself against narcissists better.

This book aimed to teach you to understand narcissism at its core as a disordered way of thinking. It discussed the key facets of narcissism, along with the behavioral habits that are dead giveaways someone is a narcissist. It discussed the difference between vulnerable and grandiose narcissists and provided identifying features of malignant narcissists. You were provided with the traits narcissists use to identify their next targets, and how narcissists in different types of relationships present themselves. The differences between male and female narcissists were emphasized. You were introduced to the basics of the most common treatments for narcissistic personality disorder, should the narcissist in your life legitimately want to better him or herself. The most effective tactics to deal with narcissists to avoid or minimize harm were provided, ranging from cutting off the narcissist to how to cope with narcissistic tendencies. Lastly, you were given a guide to the first steps in healing yourself from the abuse you endured. The information in this book will become your map to navigate the dark seas of narcissistic abuse.

Remember, underneath all of the grandiosity and confidence, at the heart of the narcissist is something so broken that it has altered his perception of the world around him. This is not an excuse for the behavior, but it becomes a bit easier to understand the desire to lash out at others if you recognize that the narcissist wants to protect himself from further harm and is inherently distrustful of people around him. By placing himself on a pedestal, he puts himself in a position of emotional invulnerability; after all, the narcissist believes you cannot hurt someone if you are inferior to him. All of his behavior has been developed as a coping mechanism against some sort of trauma, whether it was abuse, neglect, emotional neglect, or some something else. You cannot help the narcissist resolve these issues without him being willing to accept responsibility and desiring to change on his own.

As you continue on your journey of disengaging or dealing with a narcissist, remind yourself that it is okay to ask for help or support from others. Do not be afraid to contact professionals if you need help processing why you were a victim in the first place, processing the abuse, or disentangling yourself from the narcissist's grasp and influence.

Remember that you are absolutely worthy of respect, love, and happiness and that your perceptions of the world around you are likely much more accurate than the narcissist in your life wants you to believe. Congratulations on completing this book and good luck in your future endeavors with narcissists.

And one last thing, please consider leaving a review on Amazon to share your thoughts of this book.

amazon.com/review/create-review/listing

59717669R00080

Made in the USA
Middletown, DE
12 August 2019